KELLY M

AMAZING LOVE

He's coming again!
Are you ready?

Trilogy Christian Publishers

A Wholly Owned Subsidiary of Trinity Broadcasting Network

2442 Michelle Drive

Tustin, CA 92780

For information, address Trilogy Christian Publishing

Rights Department, 2442 Michelle Drive, Tustin, CA 92780.

Trilogy Christian Publishing/ TBN and colophon are trademarks of Trinity Broadcasting Network.

For information about special discounts for bulk purchases, please contact Trilogy Christian Publishing.

10 9 8 7 6 5 4 3 2 1

Library of Congress Cataloging-in-Publication Data is available.

ISBN 979-8-89041-772-5

ISBN 979-8-89041-773-2 (ebook)

TABLE OF CONTENTS

DEDICATION

I want to dedicate this book, first and foremost, to my Heavenly Father for inspiring me to write this book. One thing I know for sure is that I could have never written this book without Him. To God be the Glory!

Second, I dedicate this book to my mother and father, Nelda and Donnie Mauney, who have always been my biggest cheerleaders in encouraging me to write and publish my poems.

My dad wanted me to write this before he passed away, but sadly, I didn't accomplish that. So, this is for you, Dad; thank you for being such a great example of who Jesus is. And thank you for passing your love for the Lord down to me. We wrote the poem "The Rich Man" together, which he wanted me to write because he had such a heart for the lost.

Mom, thank you for always being a shining ray of light, peace, and joy and the sweetest woman I've ever known. A true Proverbs 31 woman.

Thank you both for taking me to church every Sunday, always being there for me, and for your unconditional love. I have truly been blessed with the best!

YOU ARE LOVED

You are loved! Doesn't that make you sigh with a smile? To know that Someone unconditionally loves you? Can this be true? Can I indeed be unconditionally loved by Someone?

God created you to hunger for this and to long for this because He wants a personal relationship with you. He wants to be the father, brother, husband, or friend you've never had. He wants to be the love of your life.

But many of us have never been taught who God is or experienced that special love.

Some have distorted God, making Him out to be some great punisher sitting in heaven, just waiting to squash you like a bug if you mess up. Usually, this is determined by your earthly father or stepfather or maybe friends or family who have mistreated you. Or maybe Satan is telling you one of his lies to keep you far away from knowing God.

I am very blessed to have had a father who loved God with all his heart, and because of his love for God and knowing that he was loved, he could love me and show me who God is. He showed me who God is by being such a great example of who Jesus is.

I always knew I had unconditional love from my father;

I have abused that love and taken it for granted many times. But I always knew that when everything in my world went upside down, I could always come home, and no matter what I had done, my dad always loved me just because I was his and for no other reason. This showed me who God was.

God created us to desire to be loved, and if we don't go to God for this and don't get it from our parents, we look for it in other things.

If you have a hole in your heart and you're searching for something to fill it to ease the pain, try searching for God. I challenge you to find out who He is. Don't take my word for it, but search Him out for yourself.

"The fear of the Lord is the beginning of knowledge, but fools despise wisdom and instruction" (Proverbs 1:7, NKJV).

The fear of the Lord doesn't mean you are so afraid of Him that you come to Him for your stay-out-of-hell insurance card, but it means that you believe what He says He will do. If He says don't do this or that, He means it because He knows that you will be hurt somehow if you do. You don't get a pass or a time-out. He tells you in His Word what will happen if you do what He tells you not to do. This is the fear of God. This is the beginning of knowledge for you when you believe and learn to hate evil.

So don't be a fool and rebuke wisdom because that will

cause you so much pain. God doesn't like to cause you pain, but because He loves you, He will do what He says He will do, even if it causes you pain. But it's up to you to receive and obey Him because Jesus will never force you to choose Him. He's just waiting patiently, hoping you will call His name.

Choose life or death; it's up to you. Jesus is life; Satan is death. What Jesus offers gives you peace and happiness that will last forever, but what Satan has to offer gives you pleasure for only a short while, and then it's gone, and when it's gone, it leaves a great big hole or emptiness in your life and creates a sadness that will surely follow.

Do you want… "Love, Joy, Peace, Patience, Kindness, Goodness, Faithfulness, Gentleness, and Self-Control. There is no law against these things" (Galatians 5:22–23, NLT). This is what Jesus gives you.

Or do you want… "sexual immorality, impurity, lustful pleasures, idolatry, sorcery, hostility, quarreling, jealousy, outbursts of anger, selfish ambition, dissension, division, envy, drunkenness, wild parties, and other sins like these. Let me tell you again, as I have before, that anyone living that sort of life will not inherit the Kingdom of God" (Galatians 5:19–21, NLT). This is what Satan has to offer you.

Jesus is love when you know that you are loved just for who you are and know that God created you just the way you are, and he stamped his approval on you before you ever came out of the womb. You don't have to change anything about your body because He loves you just the way you are, and when you realize this and honestly believe this, you can truly love yourself and love others without fear of rejection. If the world rejects you, Jesus will never abandon you. He says, "I will never leave you nor forsake you" (Hebrews 13:5, NKJV).

"There is no greater love than to lay down one's life for one's friends" (John 15:13, NLT).

Jesus did this by going to the cross to show you His Amazing Love!

Whether you know it or not…You Are Loved!

THIEF IN THE NIGHT

But know that if the master of the house had known what hour the thief would come, he would have watched and not allowed his house to be broken into. Therefore, be ready, for the Son of Man is coming at an hour you do not expect.

Matthew 24:43–44 (NKJV)

THIEF IN THE NIGHT

(This is a true story, which inspired
me to write this book.)

Many years ago,
I came home late one night,
just me and my daughter.
She kissed me and said, "Goodnight."

She looked up at me and said, half afraid,
"Mom, please come and sleep with me,
I don't know why I feel this way."

So, we locked the doors and got ready for bed.
We said our prayers and then covered our heads.
We left a light on every night.
When the light went off, it gave me a fright!

It was so dark and quiet I couldn't even see
a yard in front of or behind me.
Then all of a sudden, a flicker of light came on.
There was a man's image,
it was there and then gone!

I grabbed my daughter to pull her near,
and I prayed out loud,
"GOD, PLEASE HELP US HERE!"

For a moment, there was nothing
but silence and fear.

I could feel the man close,
I knew he was near.

At that moment, there was nothing I could do,
So I said a prayer of Love to God to help us through.
At that moment, he turned and ran
out of our house and off our land.

We jumped in the car and chased him to town
to get a license plate number,
just some way to track him down!

We came up to a policeman
who helped me calm down.
He took me back home until the sheriff came around!

We went to my parents to spend the rest of the night.
When I laid my head on my pillow,
I had another fright!
I heard the Lord say,
"That's how quickly I'll come!
Like a thief in the night,
I'll be here and then gone."

"So, if you're not ready, you need to be,
for you don't know what day or what hour
My face, you will see.
I'm sending you this message,
out of Love for you from Me!"

"So, tell everyone you possibly can,
I'm coming back soon,
this is My promise,
this is My plan."

PEOPLE GET READY

Let not your heart be troubled; you believe in God, also believe in Me. In My Father's house are many mansions; if it were not so, I would have told you. I go to prepare a place for you. And if I go and prepare a place for you, I will come again and receive you to Myself; that where I am, there you may also be.

John 14:1–3 (NKJV)

PEOPLE GET READY

What's that sound?
Do you hear it?
Do you know it?
Do you believe it?
Will you be Ready?

I know what you are thinking.
You're thinking,
What? What? What?

Do you hear the sound of Gabriel's horn
calling just for you?
Do you genuinely understand the Gospel and the truth?
Do you believe in the Resurrection?
Do you believe that Jesus will come again?
Are you watching for the signs of the end?

Jesus said to watch for the signs of His coming.
They will be everywhere.
There will be signs in the sun, moon, and the stars.
There will be famine, earthquakes,
and pestilence everywhere.

He said don't let anyone deceive you.
There will be many that come in His name.
Just be sure and put on the whole armor of God.
Pray and read your Bible every day.

You will hear about wars and rumors of wars,
but don't let this trouble you.
Nations will rise against nations and
Kingdoms will rise against kingdoms, too.

But don't be afraid. Just look up,
Jesus will be coming for you.

How do I know there's life after death?
How do I know Jesus is coming again?

Because He said when He was here on earth,
"Let not your heart be troubled;
You believe in God; also believe in Me.
In My Father's house are many mansions;
If it were not so, I would have told you.
If I go to prepare a place for you
I will come again and receive you to Myself;
That where I am, there you may also be."
He's preparing for us a mansion! Hallelujah!
We are the sons and the daughters of the King!
No more living in destitution! Praise God!
We will be Royalty!

Can you see it?
Can you believe it?
Can you receive it?
Will you be ready?

People Get Ready because Jesus is coming!
So, look up and be ready for the King!

THE THIEF'S PURPOSE

The thief does not come except to steal, and to kill, and to destroy. I have come that they may have life and that they may have it more abundantly.

John 10:10 (NKJV)

JUST ONE BITE

In the beginning, a long time ago. God created man and woman, pure and holy, don't you know? They had nothing to be ashamed of and nothing to fear, for they were perfect in every way, and God was always near.

God created a garden for them, not lacking anything; they had fresh water, food, and many beautiful things. But…there was one thing forbidden.

In the middle of this garden was a vast and beautiful tree, full of bright red, delicious apples, magnificent for the eyes to see. But man was never to touch or eat from that tree. That was the only command that God gave to Adam and Eve. Never eat from the knowledge tree. The tree of good and evil was placed there with a curse. If they ever ate from it, their lives would change for the worst. They were meant to live forever and never die. But just one bite of these apples would mean they would surely die.

But one day, while walking in the cool of the day, Eve allowed a serpent in the garden to distract her way. She could've turned and walked away; she could've passed him by, but the serpent, so evil, cunningly caught her eye. She listened very intently; she took in what he had to say. Every question she knew the answer to, but she never walked away.

The serpent plucked one of the apples and tossed it in the air; with a gleam in his eye and a plan in his heart, he offered it to Eve with an evil stare.

"Just one bite won't hurt you, for you will not surely die; come on, look at it; if anything, it will make you all-knowing and wise. God knows it will only open your eyes, so don't listen to His preposterous lies."

So, Eve thought, what could it hurt? It's so beautiful, and why would it be wrong to be wise? Then she took the fruit and ate it, and with much surprise, she offered it to her husband for his demise. Immediately, their eyes were opened, which gave them a horrible fright, afraid of what God would do to them, so they hid from his sight.

God came walking and calling out to them, even though He knew where they were, offering a chance, a hope of repentance, but no, not a word.

"Adam, where are you?" God called out.

"I heard Your voice, and I was naked and afraid, so I hid from You, afraid of what You would say."

"Who told you that you were naked? Have you eaten from that tree?" Here was his chance to confess, repent, and be set free, but not Adam; he blamed Eve.

"The woman You made gave me this terrible fruit."

The Lord God said to the woman, "What have you done?"

The woman said, "The serpent in the garden has deceived me; because of him, I ate one."

God turned and said to the serpent, "Because you have done this, you are cursed more than any cattle or beast of the field; on your belly, you shall go, and dust will be your fill. I will put hatred between you and this woman and between your seed and hers; he shall bruise your head and you, his heel. You shall always be cursed because you come only to seek, destroy and kill."

In the beginning, God created mankind to live forever; this was God's plan from the start, but one small act of disobedience condemned us to death and broke God's heart.

So, remember:

Just one bite is all it took to change this whole world.
Just one bite changed the course of every boy and girl.
Just one bite sentenced mankind to an early grave.
Just one bite sent Jesus to earth to save.
Just one bite caused Jesus to be crucified on that ugly old tree.

Could that tree of good and evil be that very same tree?

Just one bite and Jesus said, "Yes, I'll go!" He never condemned us because He loved us so. Even though it cost Him everything, He was happy to go.

So, remember, disobedience comes with a price; it might have only been once, but the outcome is never nice.

Obedience never causes any sacrifice.

Receive His love and be set free; live forever with Jesus.

What a wonderful life that will be!

Forever in His presence, just you and He!

NO ONE KNOWS THE DAY OR THE HOUR

But of that day and hour no one knows, not even the angels of heaven, but My Father only. But as the days of Noah were, so also will the coming of the Son of Man be. For as in the days before the flood, they were eating and drinking, marrying and giving in marriage, until the day that Noah entered the ark, and did not know until the flood came and took them all away, so also will the coming of the Son of Man be.

Matthew 24:36–39 (NKJV)

NOAH AND THE ARK

After man was kicked out of the garden,
the bad didn't end there.
It just got uglier and uglier with each passing year.
Lying, cheating, stealing, and murdering at their best.
The Lord saw how wicked man had become
and knew he'd never pass the test.

Every thought of man's heart was evil.
He was filled with anger and hate,
Satan had cast his fiery net, sealing man's fate.

The Lord was sorry that he made mankind,
even sadder for the angel that caused this war.
The Lord said, "I will destroy man whom I have created;
both man and beast will be no more."

But there was one man, Noah, who found grace
in the eyes of the Lord.

God said to Noah, "The end of all life
has come before me;
I can't let man go on like this anymore."
So, He sent a flood to destroy mankind,
except for what he preserved on the Ark,
Man was no more.

Are we back there again?

Are we back there staring at the Ark that Noah built?

Are we laughing, not believing the truth?
When God sealed up the door and left mankind out,
there was nothing man could do.

I believe Jesus when He said he is coming back again!

How about you?

IN THE GARDEN

In the cool of the day
walking in the garden by the waterfall
God and Jesus are strolling, admiring it all.

Then, all of a sudden, the bushes begin to shake
and out in front of them jumps Satan, the big lying snake.

Laughing and squirming, acting the fool,
he points his bony finger at Jesus, thinking,
he's so cool, says…

"Well, if it isn't God Almighty
and His precious little lamb
strutting through the Garden,
I'm sure telling all the animals
that He is the Great I am!"

"What are you doing, Satan,
and what do you want this time?"

"Oh, I'm glad you asked, Jesus;
I thought you might want to know.
I caught a net full of your people down below."

"You what?"

"Oh yeah, Jesus, Your little lambs,
the ones You love so much.
They were so busy fussing and fighting with each other
I ate them for lunch!"

"What do you want with them, Satan?
Or do you even know?"

"Oh, I'm going to have some fun with them
I'm going to teach them how to hate each other so!
I will teach them about murder, greed, lust, and strife!
Oh yeah, and most importantly, how to end their life!"

"What will you do with them
when you're through with them?"

"I want them to bow down and worship me
now and forever and for all eternity!"

"How much do you want for them?"

"Oh, You don't want those hateful, nasty little lambs.
They will spit on You and beat You in the ground."

"How much, Satan?"

"Oh, let me think…
I want it all, Jesus!
I want Your power!
I want Your glory!
I want to be the Messiah!
I want Your story!

But if I can't have all of that,
then I want Your blood!
I want You to die!
Of great humiliation
and stabbed in the side.
That's what I want!"

"Done!" Jesus says.

"Oh really? Just like that?"

"Just like that!" Jesus says.

"Well, aren't You the man?
You have yourself a deal!"

And You thought I just came to
destroy, steal, and kill!"

"Get out of here, Satan!
You think you've already won,
you forget I'm not afraid of you,
the battle has just begun."

"Well, no need to get so nasty, Jesus,
I'll call the whole thing off,
if You will get on Your knees
and beg me, pretty please.
I'll give You Your kids
at the bottom of those rocks!"

"Get out of here, Satan,
Go crawl around in the dirt!"

"Okay, I'm gone, Jesus
don't lose your shirt."

Satan leaves…

God puts His hand on Jesus' shoulder
And says, "You know what this means?"

"Yes, Father, I do!"

"Then go get our children
and bring them home, back to this garden
free from Satan's throne!"

"Don't worry, Father,
I won't be long,
I'll bring back our children!
Where they belong!"

I WONDER

So, God went searching throughout the land.
For a maiden pure and holy with just the right man.
A man who was in the house of David's family tree.
It wasn't all about Mary;
it was about Joseph, too, you see.

But each one had to be obedient and do their part,
for if they didn't, how would this ever start?

How frightening and exciting it must have been
when the Angel came to Mary and shared God's plan.
She could have said no, because who would believe?
But she denied herself and said, "Let this be unto me."

Oh, how enormous and overwhelming was this plan!
How will her family and Joseph ever understand?
And how could she be sure that what she heard was true?
The Angel told Mary, your cousin
Elizabeth is with child too.

So immediately, Mary ran to see Elizabeth
to confirm what she'd heard.
When she visited Elizabeth, the babe leaped
when Mary spoke only a word.
When the babe leaped inside, Elizabeth fell
to her knees, filled with the Holy Spirit,
and cried, "Blessed is she who believed."

Mary knew in her heart, without any
doubt, what was to be, and she wanted to shout.
She knew at that moment that she could
handle whatever came her way,
whatever people would believe, whatever they would say,
she knew that God was with her, now and always.

She knew God would handle Joseph,
and He did in a dream.
An Angel came to him and told him
not to be afraid but to believe.
To take Mary for his wife, for she will have a Son, and
you shall call him JESUS,
for He will bring Salvation to everyone.

Everyone who will choose to believe!

So, a decree went out from Caesar Augustus
that all should be registered in their city,
so Mary and Joseph left Galilee.
To the city of David, which was called Bethlehem,
Mary gave birth to Jesus, the "Great I Am!"

I wonder what Mary was thinking as she was giving birth.
Did she question her ability as a mother or her worth?
Did she think, how will I teach the
Lord of Lords and the King of Kings?

How will I ever be able to take care of all His needs?

I wonder if she knew He would die on that ugly old tree?
Surely she didn't, because that would
be too hard to conceive.

And what about Joseph?
What was going through his mind?
How will I be a father to the LORD of all mankind?

So, they packed their bags and got ready to go.
They left the ones who turned their backs
on them and curled their nose.
It was okay. They left in peace; they followed
their hearts, and in God, they believed.

When they got to Bethlehem, there was no place to stay.
Everywhere they looked, they were turned away,
but one man pointed them to a barn with
a manger and hay.

A great light was shining over the barn,
a light from heaven shown from one star.

Then, all of a sudden, when Jesus was born,
a great sound came forth from an Angel and a horn.
The Angel declared that Christ was born.

Over the mountain on camels came wise men from afar,
being oh-so faithful and obedient to
follow the beautiful star!
Gold, frankincense, and myrrh they did bring
to give to the baby Jesus, their newborn King.

The Shepherds and sheep gathered around to see
what the Angels had told them they wanted to believe!
And lo and behold, it was confirmed there was Jesus,
their newborn King!

There was a cry of excitement that filled the air!
Shouts of hallelujah, thanking God for sending Jesus…

His heir!

JOHN THE BAPTIST

John the Baptist, just who was he?

A wild man in the wilderness?
A man who wore camel's hair?
A man who ate locusts and honey?
Yes, to all of these!

But he also had a great call on his life
that sometimes caused him pain and great strife.
But John did not care; he knew who he was.
He was chosen by God; he knew he was loved.

He was a great Prophet, sent from above.
The front-runner for Jesus Christ,
whom he dearly loved.

He opened the hearts of man so they could see.
He cried, "Repent, turn from your sins,
prepare for the coming King!

The prophet Malachi said that before John was born
God would send another prophet like Elijah
before the great and dreadful day of the Lord.

His preaching would bring fathers and
children back together again,
but if they did not repent, God would destroy their land.

People from all over Judea went out to the
wilderness to hear him preach,

and when they confessed their sins to him,
he baptized them in the Jordan River
as a sign that they were clean.

Pharisees and Sadducees came out to be baptized,
but when he saw them, he stopped them
and uncovered their lies.

"You sons of snakes!" He warned them.
"Who said that you could escape
the coming wrath of God?
Do you think being baptized or being a Jew
will keep you safe?
And you think I'm odd?

"Before I baptize you,
prove that you have turned from your sins
by doing good deeds, one to another,
for God sees what lies within.
"He knows what you've done to your brother.
For even now, the ax of God's judgment
is poised to cut the unproductive trees down.
So, check and see if there's good fruit from your trees.
If not, they will be chopped and burned to the ground.

"With water, I baptize those who repent of their sins;
but there is another who comes baptizing
with the Holy Spirit and fire.
He will separate the chaff from the grain,
burning the chaff with never-ending fire.

"So, repent, turn from your sins,
prepare to meet Jesus, the coming King.

THE RICH MAN

There once was a rich man dressed in
purple and fine linen
who lived with all the pleasures this world had given!
He was happy all day;
he didn't care what people had to say.
He was harsh; he was cold; he was uncaring.

At the Rich man's gate,
there was a beggar man named Lazarus,
whom the rich man began to hate.

Lazarus was covered with sores;
to the rich man, Lazarus was disgusting,
someone he abhorred!

There was so much good the Rich man could've done
to spare a morsel, just a crumb,
But no, not the rich man.
He never gave him one.

But then, one day, an Angel took the beggar man away
to Heaven, where he belonged.
He had no more sores on his head,
no sorrows or worry about being fed.
Instead, he was happy and blessed; he was finally living!

But during this time, the Rich man had died
and was taken to Hell from the grave.
He had everything this world could bring

except what money couldn't buy.
It was Jesus Christ he had denied.

He was happy living his way until he was taken away
to a place called Hades, called Hell.
It was smoldering hot, and he was tormented a lot;
So, he prayed, "Oh, Dear Lord, why couldn't I see?"

Immediately, his eyes opened wide,
and he saw the beggar, Lazarus, by Abraham's side.
And begged, "Please have mercy on me!"

But Abraham said, "No, it's too late; you must go
to this place called Hell that you've chosen."

The Rich man cried, "Please, come and rescue me;
tell Lazarus to dip his finger
in the water to cool my tongue."

Again, Abraham said, "No, you can't cross over to go;
your fate has been sealed. It's over."

"Then one more thing, I plead, send Lazarus for me,
to tell my family and my friends there is a Hell."

Abraham replied, "They have Moses
and the Prophets at their side;
Let them go and listen to them."

The Rich man said, "No,
if someone from the dead doesn't go,
I'm afraid they won't repent; they won't listen."

"If they don't listen to them," Abraham told him,

"the dead won't change their mind or convince them!"

So, Jesus, what do we do? What do we say?
When people's hearts are so hardened, they turn away.

We must point them to You; pray for them too.
For You went to the cross for this reason.
So that no one should die (eternally),
believe Satan's lie,
and live forever in a fiery furnace.

We must tell our family and friends
that Jesus is coming back again!

Nobody knows when!
Choose life or death!

The End!

GO AND SIN NO MORE

Jesus was at the Temple speaking to the crowd,
when all of a sudden, the scribes and Pharisees
brought a woman in,
and they threw her on the ground.
"This woman was caught in adultery.
The Law of Moses says she must pay.
It says that we must stone her,
but Jesus, what do you have to say?"

They said this to test Jesus,
hoping to set a trap to push Him in,
but He didn't take their bait. He just stooped down
and wrote something in the sand.

They continued asking Him,
demanding to know His thoughts,
when gently He stood and turned to them, saying,
"He who is without sin among you throw the first rock."

Then Jesus stooped back down on the ground,
continuing to write in the sand,
not saying anything but one by one,
they all laid their rocks down.

I wonder what Jesus might have written in the sand;
was He revealing each of their crimes?
Whatever He wrote, there was a reason,
for they were convicted and changed their minds.

Then Jesus stood up when the men were gone
and turned to the woman to say,
"Woman, where are your accusers?
Is there anyone to condemn you today?"

She said, "No one, Lord."

Then Jesus told her,
"Neither do I condemn you;
now go and sin no more."

What just happened? She had to have thought.
She was fixing to die, but now she's not.
She was set free from her guilt and shame.
It happened so fast. Did she even get His name?
She was dirty, but now she was clean.
She was forgiven by this Man from Galilee.

Jesus turned and spoke to the crowd, saying,
"I am the light of the world.
He who follows Me shall not walk in darkness
but have the light of life."

But the Pharisees didn't believe Him;
they wanted to cause Him strife.

But I bet the woman caught in adultery believed Him.

Because now she had a new life!

JESUS HEALS THEM ALL

Jesus traveled through Galilee
teaching about the Good News everywhere,
in the synagogues and hillsides,
large crowds gathered here and there.

The word of God captured them.
The truth opened their hearts to receive.
They received God's goodness and mercy.
All they had to do was believe.

He healed everyone who asked Him;
A leper asked and received,
"If you want to, you can heal me."
Jesus said, "I want to! Be healed."
And the Leper was clean.

When Jesus arrived in Capernaum,
a Roman soldier met Him at the door
to heal his servant boy, who was paralyzed
and in great pain like never before.

Jesus said, "Yes, I will come and heal him."
But the soldier replied, "No,
for I am not worthy of having you where I reside.
But if you say, right here, right now,
be healed, I know it's done!
I know you speak with authority,
so whatever you say shall be done!"

With great admiration for this man's faith,
Jesus said, "Go on home. What you have believed is done!
Your servant boy is healed this very moment;
the victory is his. He has won."

When Jesus arrived at Peter's house,
Peter's mother-in-law was sick inside.
She was lying in bed with a high fever,
and Jesus immediately went to her side.
He reached out his hand and touched her,
and immediately the fever was gone.
She jumped out of bed, not missing a step,
and said their dinner was on.

That evening, they brought the demon-possessed.
When Jesus saw them, He set them free.
He spoke one word to the demons inside,
and they left without a plea.

A rabbi from a local church came to worship Him.
He said, "My little daughter has just died,
but if you come, she will live again."
So Jesus rose and went with the Rabbi.
When he arrived at the Rabbi's home,
there was a great noise inside;
the music and the funeral march;
Jesus cast all the people aside.
He said for all to get out, for she was not dead but asleep.
They all scoffed and sneered at Him
as they got up to leave.

After they had left the room,

He reached out to touch the little girl's hand.
Immediately she arose and was all right again!
As Jesus left the little girl's home,
two blind men followed behind
shouting, "O Son of King David, have mercy on us."
Then they went into the house where He resided.

Jesus asked them, "Do you believe I can make you see?"
And they said, "Yes, Lord, we certainly do."
So, he told them, "Because of your faith, it shall be done.
Your eyes will be brand new."

Jesus called out His twelve disciples
and gave them authority.
Tell the people that the Kingdom of Heaven
is near when you leave.
Heal the sick, raise the dead, cure the lepers
and every sickness and disease.

Give as freely as you have received.
Believe, and it shall be.
Only go to my lost sheep, for they are the ones in need.

I believe He has commissioned us all to do these things.
With the help of the Holy Spirit, people can be set free.
So be ready when He calls to use your hands and feet,
For someone is waiting for you in their time of need.

Don't be afraid wherever you go.
For God will never leave you nor forsake you,
for the Bible tells us so!

Just say yes when God says, "Go!"

LAZARUS, MARTHA, AND MARY

Do you remember Mary and Martha,
the sisters of Lazarus?

Martha was a servant who loved to prepare
great meals and serve her folks,
But Mary was a seeker of God who loved to sit and soak.

While Martha was in the kitchen preparing every meal,
Mary was at Jesus' feet, getting her daily fill.
Eating on the word of God as Jesus told a story.
She was hanging onto every word
while Martha was in her glory.

Martha would get so mad at Mary for
not helping her prepare,
but Mary didn't even hear her because Jesus was there.
Martha said to Jesus, "Lord, do you not care
that my sister has left me all alone to serve and prepare?"

"Martha, Martha, you are troubled about so many things,
while Mary is sitting at my feet preparing for her wings."

So, Jesus left and went on His way
to heal the sick and the blind
when one day, a messenger came to Him saying that
Lazarus was sick and it may be his time.

But when Jesus heard this message,

He said this sickness would not end in death.
This has happened for a reason,
so God will get the glory from this.

Even though Jesus loved Martha, Mary, and Lazarus,
He stayed away for two more days.
Could it be to show the people how it would be
when Jesus died and was raised?

Then Jesus said to His disciples,
"Our friend Lazarus has fallen asleep,
so now I will go and wake him up.
Come, let's go and see."

When Jesus arrived at Bethany, He was told Lazarus had
been dead and in his grave for four days. When Martha
heard that Jesus was coming, she met Him on His way.

She said, "Lord, if only You had been here,
my brother would still be alive,
but even so, I know God will give
You whatever You decide."

Jesus told her, "Your brother will rise."

"Yes, I know that Lazarus will again rise in the
resurrection on the very last day.
No matter how it looks, no matter what people might say."

Jesus said, "I am the resurrection and the life.
Though he may die, he who believes in Me shall live.
Do you believe, Martha,
that whoever lives and believes in Me shall never die?"

"Yes, Lord, I believe You are the Son of God;
You are the Christ!"
Then Martha went on her way and
called out to Mary to say,
"The Teacher has come and is calling for you;
go to Him now; go to Him soon."

When Mary heard this, she quickly rose
and ran out of the house and down the road.
When Mary found Jesus, she fell at His feet. She didn't
even realize the Jews were following her down the street.

She cried to Jesus, saying, "Lord, if You had been here,
my brother would not have died."

Jesus said, "Where have you laid him?"
as He groaned in the spirit and cried.

Some Jews mumbled to each other, "Couldn't this Man,
who opened blind eyes, have taken the time to see to His
friend and try to keep him alive?"

Then Jesus, again groaning into Himself, came to the
tomb and said, "Roll the stone away."

Immediately, Martha cried out, "Oh Lord, he's been dead
now for four days; the smell must be unbearable.
Isn't there any other way?"

Jesus said, "Did I not say that if you believed, you would
see the Glory of God? So stand back and receive;
don't look as if this was odd."

So, they took away the stone from the place where the
dead man, Lazarus, lay,
and Jesus lifted His eyes, and the people heard Him say,
"Father, I thank You for always hearing Me; I pray that
they will know that it was You who sent Me;
it was You who told me when to go."

"Lazarus, come forth!" Jesus said with a shout.
Immediately, the man wrapped in grave clothes came out!
"Loose him and let him go free."

Lazarus was dead, but now he's alive!

Do you believe?

JUDAS

Wouldn't you hate the thought of being Judas?
Oh, how quickly we seem to judge.
Oh, I would have never done that to Jesus,
but now you, I'm not sure, as you point and nudge.

Judas was very materialistic; greed was his first crime.
That's how he opened the door to the devil.
Because money was on his mind.

What set him off toward Jesus
was when Mary, Lazarus' sister,
brought perfume to anoint Him.
Judas knew how expensive this bottle was
and snatched it from her hand.

"That perfume was worth a fortune," Judas said.
"It should have been sold
and the money given to the poor."

Jesus replied, "Let her alone. She did it for my burial;
you can always help the poor."
Then Judas turned and walked out the door.

This reply made Judas angry, which was his second crime.
God hates unrighteous anger because it clouds your
judgment and messes with your mind.

You will eventually hurt someone you love in time.
Just like Judas did!

Judas stormed out of the door in anger
because of Jesus' reply.
He didn't even hear what Jesus said,
that soon he would die.
No, all he could hear was Satan and his great lie.

So, Judas went to the chief priests and asked,
"How much will you pay me to put Jesus in your hands?"
And for only thirty silver coins,
Judas waited for the opportunity to betray Him.

Jesus called him out at the Passover meal,
saying, "One of you will betray Me."

Each disciple gasped and searched their
hearts, asking, "Is it me?"

Jesus shared with His disciples how bad this would be,
for whoever did this terrible crime should never be.
Maybe He was allowing Judas the opportunity
to turn and repent, but Judas didn't do this,
and away Jesus sent...Judas.

Jesus and the disciples, after finishing their meal,
went out into the garden to pray, and He revealed.

"Tonight, you will all desert me. For it is written in the
Scriptures that God will smite the Shepherd, and the flock
will flee. But after I have been brought back to life,
I will meet you in Galilee."

Peter declared, "If everyone else deserts you, Lord,
I promise I will not."

But Jesus told him, "The truth is that this very night
before the cock crows at dawn,
you will have denied Me three times.
Three times you will turn and run!"

"I would die first!" Peter insisted,
and the disciples said the same.
Then Jesus went on into the garden
to pray and ease His pain.

To a place called Gethsemane,
He took His disciples to pray.
Further into the garden,
He took Peter and the two sons of Zebedee
and said, "My soul is exceedingly sorrowful,
even to death.
So, stay here and watch with Me."

Three times, Jesus went off to pray,
and three times He found Peter
and the other two had drifted away.

Each time, He said, "Watch and pray,
lest you enter into temptation.
The spirit indeed is willing, but the flesh is weak."

If Peter had stayed awake with Jesus and prayed,
would he have betrayed Him that very same day?
Jesus was trying to help him prepare for what was ahead,
but the flesh wasn't willing. He ran instead.

Then, after praying for the third time,
Judas came to betray Him.

With a large crowd following with swords and clubs,
he turned Jesus over to them.

This was Judas' third crime; he helped
sentence Jesus to die.
He opened the door to Satan and swallowed his great lie.

Sin clouded his vision with anger and greed
so much that it consumed him until he couldn't see.
He took the money back, but it was too late.
So, he hung himself, determining his fate.

Three times, he sinned against Jesus.
And three times, Peter did the same
But three times, Jesus forgave Peter,
restoring his good name.

I wonder…what if Judas had turned from his sins and
asked Jesus to forgive him?
Would he have been forgiven,
even though Jesus still died?
Would he be in heaven today, by Jesus' side?

I wonder?

THE PASSOVER

I believe the Passover started a long time ago
with a man called Moses and a King named Pharaoh.

God sent Moses to Pharaoh to tell him to
"Let My People Go!"

The Israelites, whom Pharaoh
held in bondage to build his city.
But Pharaoh said, "No!"

It took ten plagues from God to bring Pharaoh around.
The tenth one put Pharaoh's firstborn son in the ground.

All the firstborns in Egypt were cursed to die.
If they didn't have the lamb's blood on their doorpost,
the Death Angel would not pass them by.

But the Israelites did, and they were all set free,
then Pharaoh called Moses and told them to leave.

"Go worship your God and take your cattle and sheep
just go now, but first, bless me."

So, Pharaoh finally let God's People Go
through the Passover, the blood,
and the death of the lamb.
The people were back with God, the Great I Am!

Until...
One day, Satan cast his fiery net
and captured God's people again.

One by one, year by year, they quit holding God dear.
You would think that we, the people, would remember!

First, it was Adam and Eve.
Then, Noah and the High Seas.
Then, the death of the firstborn with Pharaoh.
Then, Satan came along, challenging God's only Son
to fight for the lives of God's people.

So, God sent Jesus, His Son, His perfect, spotless lamb
to be crucified on the Cross for our sins.
To be nailed to that tree (the doorpost)
so that we could be freed
by His blood that flowed down from the Cross.

Spotless and clean is how we would be seen
so that the Death Angel would pass us by.

So, again, Satan let God's People Go
through the Passover, the blood,
and the death of the lamb.
The people were back with God, the Great I Am!

So, when you take Communion, the Passover meal,
you now will understand why.

When you take the bread, the bread of life,
His body that He gave for you
that was beaten and scourged.
He said not a word
so that His stripes would now heal you.

Do this in remembrance of Him.

When you drink from the cup, the New Covenant,
His blood, which He shed for you,
You're putting His blood on your doorpost
so that the Death Angel will pass by you.

Do this in remembrance of Him.

GO AHEAD
AND CRUCIFY ME

They're coming, Heavenly Father,
they're coming to take Me away.
I see the light in the distance, and it makes Me sad,
for I know Judas is leading the way.

He just sealed the deal with a kiss on My face,
a kiss that might as well say,
I did my job; Jesus is yours,
Now pay me my earnings, my wage.

The wages of sin are death, my friend,
I wish it could have been another way.
But now it's done, but death hasn't won,
for I will arise again in three days.

"Whom are you seeking?" I asked them.

"Jesus of Nazareth," they say.

"I am He, now that you have Me,
let My people go their own way."

With torches and weapons, they bound Me,
taking Me to Caiaphas, the high priest.
My people are gone. No, there is one,
and Peter walks very discreet.

The scribes and the elders are assembled,

they seek to destroy Me.
To put Me to death, to yell, crucify
and nail Me to that old rugged tree.
But little do they know that whatever they do,
they have no power over Me.

They're sending Me on to Pilate.
Go ahead and carry Me.
I have two thousand angels beside Me,
I can call them to charge with one plea.
But that's not why I've come here to earth.
So go ahead and crucify Me.

Now Pilate questions the people,
"What evil has this man done?"

With the crowd rising in numbers, shouting,
"Release Barabbas, the prisoner,
and crucify this Holy One!"

So, Pilate turns Me over to the people,
knowing that he could not prevail.
He washes his hands of innocent blood,
as if this would avail.

Oh, help Me, Heavenly Father,
they're grabbing and pulling Me.
They're spitting in My face,
ripping My clothes,
sending Me to be scourged,
and putting a crown of thorns in its place.

If only they could understand,

I just want their love and embrace.

I know that I can do this,
I know that You're here with Me.
I know I have to do this
for all the world to see.

To see how much We love them,
to see them all set free.
To not be slaves of death and Hell
but to live forever free with You and Me.

So, go ahead, people, do what you must,
I'll lift My head and carry My Cross
for I am already free!

So, go ahead and crucify Me!

DOWN CALVARY ROAD

Today there was a battle.
None as I'd ever seen.
As Jesus walked down Calvary Road,
the crowd became hateful and mean.

I prayed to God to open my eyes
to see what was going on,
immediately, the scales fell off
and I could see the battle raging on.

As Jesus walked down Calvary Road
the demons walked beside Him, punching the crowd,
riling them up, pouring hate and evil inside.

The angels were on the other side of Jesus,
walking and listening as the crowd cried, "Crucify!"
Why weren't they doing something?
Why wouldn't they lift a hand?
As Jesus walked down that dusty road.
What was the matter with them?

I don't understand, dear Jesus,
You could stop this with one shout or command.
What was driving You onto the Cross?
How much can one man stand?

At that moment, it was like He could read my thoughts.
He turned and looked me in the eye.
As a tear rolled down His blood-stained face,

He said, "My child, please do not cry.

"I know it doesn't seem like it now,
but I am doing this for you.
The devil and demons think they have won,
but they can't win if they don't have you.

"I'm going to be with my Heavenly Father
as soon as this is done.
I want you there beside Me,
when your time on Earth is done.

"Sometimes walking with the crowd
is easier than following Me.
But the crowd will only take you down
to a death where you no longer see.
But life with Me is eternal.
More blessings and love than you know.
A peace that passes all understanding,
and joy wherever you go!

"Today looks hopeless and hurtful.
But tomorrow, I'll be set free
of the chains of Hell and destruction.
My prayer is that one day you'll be with Me.

"Tell all your friends and family
what is going on here…

"Tell them the angels are walking beside them,
just as they are with Me today.
All you have to do is speak,
and immediately they obey.

They can't do anything unless you ask them,
so don't be afraid.

"Now let Me finish My journey,
for so many need Me today.
There's a thief on a cross up ahead.
Who's waiting to go with Me,
who wants to choose life instead of death,
so please don't cry for Me.

"I'm happy to do this for you
and anyone who wants to be free.
I gladly choose to serve you;
will you and your house serve Me?

"One day, this all will fade away.
One day, the choice will be gone.
The option will always be yours to make,
I hope you don't wait too long.
I hope you know how much I love you.
There's nothing that you could ever do
to keep Me from going to the Cross
and keep Hell far away from you.

"So, take up your cross and follow Me,
or let Me carry yours?
I'm always here beside you."

Sincerely,
Forever Yours!

WHY?

Why, oh why, LORD, did You have to die?
I miss You so much; I want to cry.
I wanted to help You; oh Lord, how I tried,
but I could do nothing as You passed by.

Oh friend, what is that you say?
Do you want to know what happened here today?

Well…

Today we buried Jesus; they put thorns upon His head.
They buried them deep into His brow until He bled.

He carried that heavy wooden cross,
heavy-laden upon His back,
walking down that dusty road,
never looking back.
Never looking back to see.
Where are My friends?
Why have they deserted Me?

Why did He do it?
Why did He have to die?
Were we worth the sacrifice?

How can He love us when all we can do is hate?
How can He forgive us, no matter what our fate?
He healed the lame; He made the blind see,
but that wasn't enough for all to believe.

They still wanted to hurt Him, to put Him in the ground.
To make Him pay for all He had done,
isn't that profound?

They laughed as they nailed Him to that old rugged tree.
They pierced His side to see if He would bleed.
Was that supposed to set us free?

You know it did!

The blood He spilled on Calvary
was spilled so that we could be set free.

We don't have to go to the altar to slay
a lamb for its blood to take our sins away.
No, Jesus was that Lamb today
that was beaten and crucified and then taken away.

But I'll never forget what He had to say
down Calvary Road when He looked my way.
He said, "Don't weep for Me because I know
into my father's house is where I'll go.

"I know where I'm going and where My journey will end.
Do you know where the road you're on will end?

"Weep for yourselves, your children, and your friends
because one day, I'll be back again.
And on that day, there will be no turning back,
it's Heaven or Hell!
Where will you be at?"

Oh, Friend, what are you waiting for?
Why can't you see? How easy it is to be set free!

No doing good works or this or that.
All you have to say is, forgive me, Lord,
come into my heart.
Yes, I want that!

So, remember today and what Jesus went through,
but please understand that in three days,
He will arise and be brand New!

Everything He did, there was a reason why.
Everything He did was for you and I.
One day, we will meet Him in the sky,
forever renewed; now you know why.
Why Jesus had to die.

He did it for you and I!

HE'S ALIVE

Hello, it's me, John!
I'm a follower of Jesus Christ.
I'm sitting here wondering,
what has happened?
How can this be?
Is Jesus now gone from me?

He was just here a few days ago, sharing His love.
Today He is gone...gone up above?
So little time
and so much to share.
How can one Man take on so much to bear?

How can You love people so much that You bleed?
How can His Love set the captives free?

How can one Man take my sins from me?
It happened so quickly; God, please help me to see.

The Thief on the cross, an ungodly man,
reached out to Jesus and made a stand.
He had the nerve to ask, "Jesus, Remember me."
I thought there was no way he would ever be set free.

But when I looked at Jesus,
even though He was so broken inside.
He looked at the Thief and began to cry.
He said your sins are forgiven.
You will be with Me

in Paradise, with My Father
one day soon, you will see.

Jesus was punished because He couldn't hate,
because He loves people more than His fate!

God so loved the world that He gave Jesus to set us free.
Even the Thief on the Cross, who said, "Remember me!"
Jesus looked up to Heaven and said it was finished!
The battle is over; death is diminished.
How empty and hollow I felt right then,
surely, Jesus, this isn't the end?

You raised people from the dead.
You opened blind eyes.
Why did you leave us?
Why did you close your eyes?

Wait one minute!

What's that sound?

Good grief, it's Mary Magdalene trying to knock the door
down!

What is she saying?

Is she screaming something about the Lord?

She's weeping and laughing with a sparkle in her eye.

"It's Jesus," Mary says.

"He's Alive!"

GETTING LEFT BEHIND

The Parable of the Wise and Foolish Virgins

Then the kingdom of heaven shall be likened to ten virgins who took their lamps and went out to meet the bridegroom. Now five of them were wise, and five were foolish. Those who were foolish took their lamps and took no oil with them, but the wise took oil in their vessels with their lamps. But while the bridegroom was delayed, they all slumbered and slept.

And at midnight a cry was heard: "Behold, the bridegroom is coming; go out to meet him!" Then all those virgins arose and trimmed their lamps. And the foolish said to the wise, "Give us some of your oil, for our lamps are going out." But the wise answered, saying, "No, lest there should not be enough for us and you; but go rather to those who sell, and buy for yourselves." And while they went to buy, the bridegroom came, and those who were ready went in with him to the wedding, and the door was shut.

Afterward, the other virgins came also, saying, "Lord, Lord, open to us!" But he answered and said, "Assuredly, I say to you, I do not know you."

Watch, therefore, for you know neither the day nor the hour in which the Son of Man is coming.

Matthew 25 1–13 (NKJV)

BRIDE OF CHRIST

Here we are, ready and waiting
for the bridegroom to return.
Dressed in our white lace and fine linen
and our lamps filled with oil to be burned.

Our floors are swept,
our closets are clean,
our hearts are filled with love,
because we don't know the date or the hour
the bridegroom will descend from above!

So, we're ready
when we hear the cry ring out,
"The bridegroom is on His way,"
to take us to the Wedding Banquet
to feast with Him on that Glorious Day!

Wait…one minute, can you hear it?
Oh, my goodness, can it be?
The Midnight cry that Jesus promised?
Is that Gabriel on his horn, calling for you and me?

Are my floors swept?
Are my closets clean?
Are my friends and family
going home with Jesus and me?
There's no time to ask; I should've made sure;
there's no looking back,

I pray they endure.

I was so sure of myself in my little world,
now the time has come.
God, please bring my son and my sweet baby girl.
I don't want them and their families to be left behind,
in this cruel world alone, so cold and unkind.

So, my friend, don't act as if you believe
what Jesus said is true.
Believe in your heart what Jesus said, He will do.
Make sure that your friends and family are ready too.
Because it will happen one day, and you know it's true!

That is…If Christ's love is in you, you do!

THE COMING OF THE SON OF MAN

Immediately after the tribulation of those days, the sun will be darkened, and the moon will not give its light; the stars will fall from heaven, and the powers of the heavens will be shaken. Then the sign of the Son of Man will appear in heaven, and then all the tribes of the earth will mourn, and they will see the Son of Man coming on the clouds of heaven with power and great glory. And He will send

His angels with a great sound of a trumpet, and they will gather together His elect from the four winds, from one end of heaven to the other.

Matthew 24:29–31 (NKJV)

Then two men will be in the field: one will be taken and the other left. Two women will be grinding at the mill: one will be taken and the other left. Watch, therefore, for you do not know what [g]hour your Lord is coming.

Matthew 24:40–42 (NKJV)

THE BEGINNING OF THE END

Cars are crashing into one another,
planes dive bombing from the air.
Trains piling up, running off the rails,
chaos, and destruction are everywhere.

In the streets, people are running frantically,
searching for their children that were once there.
Dogs running loose trying to find their masters,
fire and smoke fill the air.

There's Panic in the people's hearts
as they search and scramble to understand,
asking for help and answers.
Where are my loved ones?
Where are my friends?

A TV News Reporter steps up to ask questions
as people pass him by.
One by one, he asks them,
hoping to find some answers
to the question,

Why?

He stops a young woman and asks her,
"What is going on?"

She says with panic in her heart,
"I don't know, but my children are gone!"

The Reporter is wheeled around by a gust of wind;
it's a young man passing by.
He shouts from his skateboard,
"It's got to be Aliens!
Look Up! Watch the sky!"

Scratching his head,
the Reporter says, "Aliens?
For some reason, that doesn't seem right."

An Older woman is ambling toward him
with sadness across her face.
The Reporter says, "Ma'am, please excuse me,
but do you have any answers
about what's going on in this place?"

She says, "Yes, son, I'm afraid that I do,"
with a tear running down her face.

He says, "Great!
What are your thoughts on the disappearances?
Please tell me. I want to know!"

"My husband, who is now among the missing,
told me time and time again
that I need to ask God for His forgiveness!
That I need to be born again!
To receive Jesus Christ as my Lord and Savior,
for one day, He's coming again!

"But I never got what he was saying.
I laughed and called him an old fool,
but the old fool wasn't he; it was me!

"Now he's gone to be with Jesus,
and I'm left here all alone.
The punishment for my disbelief
is more than I can own.
For I know what lies ahead."

The Reporter says, "What lies ahead?
Please tell me. I want to know!
Please don't hold back; I'm waiting…fire away…Go!"

"Well," she sighs, "the Anti-Christ,
the Son of Satan, will soon be set free.
To run loose, to cause havoc on earth,
to bind and deceive.
If you receive his mark, you may be left alone.
But when you die, God can't save you.
It's to Hell you go.

"If you don't take his mark and say no to him,
you will lose your life, and there's no mercy in him.
Death will be something you can't even imagine!
But if you receive Jesus Christ, you will win.
But it won't be easy to stay alive or hide
from the Anti-Christ until the end.

"I'm sorry, son, but this is just the beginning of the end.
I wish we'd all been ready and had gone with Him!"

The Reporter looks up to the camera
and says,
"Cut, Cut!"

"The End!"

WORTHY IS THE LAMB

When Jesus comes home,
He places a white robe on
the ones that came with Him.

Then, they each bow down,
and He places a crown
that shows how each one has lived.

He looks up the stairs and sees God there
sitting on His throne.
With a great big smile, He passes through the aisle
and all His children bow down before Him.

They sing praises to His name
and start worshiping Him,
crying, "Worthy is the Lamb."

He passes through them all.
In His long white robe
as He climbs to the top of the stairs
where God is sitting on His throne.
He places a crown on…Jesus.

The "King of Kings and Lord of Lords."

Jesus looks to God and points down below
to his children that He's brought home.

"Father, look down below.
I've brought Our children home!

They're free from the Anti-Christ and the False Prophet!"

"Well done, My Son.
I'm so pleased with You!
Thank You for bringing them home!
Were You able to bring them all home?"

Jesus bows His head with a tear in His eye
and sadly says, "No!"

"There were so many, Father, I had to leave.
They never chose life over death.
They never would believe and, in their hearts, receive.
So now they're left unprotected with death.
They're being hunted day and night,
trying to fight the good fight.

Not to take the mark of the beast.
I pray they make it through
and come home to Me and You.
Oh, Father God, how this breaks My heart."

With a tear running down his beautiful face,
God puts His hand on Jesus' shoulder and says,
"Well, that's all You can do,
is share the truth
and honor what they decide.

"We can't make them come home.
So, they're now on their own.
There's nothing more We can do but wait.

"But for now, dry your eyes and look below

let's celebrate the ones who freely chose

to come home to live with you and me.

Let's Celebrate! Let's have a wedding feast,

for the Bridegroom and His Bride are home."

SEVEN YEARS LATER

Seven Years later
the Great Tribulation period is over.
The seven long years have come and gone
where Satan, the Anti-Christ,
and the False Prophet
believe that they have won.

But then there's God,

sitting in His garden
with Jesus by His side
enjoying Their people
both far and wide.

When…

Two Angels of God's armies bring the Anti-Christ
and his False Prophet in chains.
Everyone is whispering and pointing at them,
calling them names.

The first Angel speaks up and says,
"King of Kings and Lord of Lords.
We have captured the Anti-Christ and his False Prophet.
What shall we do with them?"

The Anti-Christ, squirming like the snake he is, says,
"Now Jesus, okay, so you've won!
What's the harm in a bit of competition?

It's just clean fun.
The battle is over, Jesus!
Let's shake hands!
What do you say?"

Jesus turns to the Angels and says,
"Take them and throw them into the Lake of Fire,
I don't want to hear anything about what they desire."

"Now, Jesus, let's talk about this.
You're supposed to be all about mercy and grace.
I'm not feeling it, Jesus.
Where's the smile on Your face?"

"Guards, take them away!"

The first Angel pushes open the door
that says the Lake of Fire or Hell.
All you see is a fire blazing and smell a horrible smell.

"Hey, wait, no, wait, this isn't right.
You can't do this, Jesus; it was a fair fight!"

The first Angel shoves him
through the door chains and all.
And all you hear is the Anti-Christ screaming,
"This isn't ALL!"

The second Angel takes the False Prophet up to the door
and the False Prophet begins to holler,
"Wait, Jesus; that old Devil made me do it,
I promise I won't run with him anymore!
I told him no, but he just…Wait…oh No…"

he cries as the Angel shoves him through the door!

Then, the second Angel nodded to Jesus
and dusted off his hands.
The crowd begins shouting and cheering, saying,
"Worthy is the Lamb!
Hallelujah, thank You, Jesus, Jesus is Lord!"

AMEN

JESUS REIGNS FOR A THOUSAND YEARS

An angel came down from heaven,
having a key to the bottomless pit.
Grabbed ahold of Satan, that old dragon
and bound him and said this is it.

For a thousand years, he'll be shut up,
while the Saints reign with Christ.
Then, after those thousand years
Satan will be released to fight his last fight.

So, for a thousand years,
Jesus will reign with those who are alive
and who lost their lives through the tribulation.

Who proclaimed God's Word;
and shared what they heard
of Jesus Christ and His salvation.

Those who did not receive the mark of the beast
on their forehead or their hands
will be brought back to life
to reign with Jesus Christ.
For the next one thousand years.

Now, a thousand years have come and gone
and Satan is released again.
He still thinks he can beat Jesus.

He still thinks he can win.

He will go out to deceive the nations of the world.
He will gather them together for his last battle.
He will seek to destroy Jerusalem and God's people,
but God will take him out with heavenly fire.

This time, he's thrown into the Lake of Fire
with the Anti-Christ and the False Prophet.
Where he will be tormented day and night
for the rest of his life,
and there is nothing he can do to stop it!

It's the end for him; hallelujah! God wins!
And we live forever and ever with Jesus!

THE SON OF MAN WILL JUDGE THE NATIONS

When the Son of Man comes in His glory, and all the holy angels with Him, then He will sit on the throne of His glory. All the nations will be gathered before Him, and He will separate them one from another, as a shepherd divides his sheep from the goats. And He will set the sheep on His right hand, but the goats on the left. Then the King will say to those on His right hand, "Come, you blessed of My Father, inherit the kingdom prepared for you from the foundation of the world."

Matthew 25:31–34 (NKJV)

101

Then He will also say to those on the left hand, "Depart from Me, you cursed, into the everlasting fire prepared for the devil and his angels."

Matthew 25:41 (NKJV)

These will go away into everlasting punishment, but the righteous into eternal life.

Matthew 25:46 (NKJV)

THE NEW JERUSALEM

Hello, it's me, John, Jesus' disciple.
I want to tell you what lies ahead.
The future looks great for God's people.
So don't be afraid of what's being said.

I saw a new earth and a new sky,
for the present was now gone.
I saw the Holy City Called the New Jerusalem,
coming down from the Heaven of God.

What a glorious sight.
I wish you could have seen it.
Like a beautiful bride on her wedding day.

It's the home, and the throne of God filled with His Glory.
It shines and glows like a precious gem.
On the foundation and walls, he tells His story
of the men who followed Him.

God's coming down to live with his people.
Where there will be no more tears,
no more death and no more pain.
Forever and ever, it will all be gone
for nothing old will remain.

For God is making all things brand new.
He is the Alpha and the Omega
the beginning and the end.
A gift he's giving to you.

But for all of those who are unfaithful
the corrupt, the murderers, the immoral,
those conversing with demons,
idol worshipers and liars.
Will all go to Hell, The Lake of Fire.

Nothing evil will ever be permitted there
in The New City, The New Jerusalem.
Only those whose names are written
in the Lamb's Book of Life will be there!

There will be a river of pure Water.
Clear as crystal flowing from the throne
coursing down the center of the main street.
And on each side, the trees of life will grow.
There will be no night there.
No need for lamps or the sun.
For the Lord God will be the light
for everyone.

Jesus said, "I am coming soon,
and with me will be my reward.
To repay everyone according to
the deeds he has done.

For he is the Alpha and The Omega
the beginning and the end.
Blessed are those who believe.

Who is washing their robes to have the right
to enter through the city gates
and eat from the Tree of Life.

Is your name in the Lamb's Book of Life?

Jesus said, "Yes, I am coming back soon!"

May the grace of our Lord Jesus Christ be with you!

GOD'S AMAZING LOVE

For God so loved the world that He gave His only begotten Son, that whoever believes in Him should not perish but have everlasting life. For God did not send His Son into the world to condemn the world, but that the world through Him might be saved.

He who believes in Him is not condemned; but he who does not believe is condemned already, because he has not believed in the name of the only begotten Son of God.

JOHN 3:16–18 (NKJV)

AMAZING LOVE

Never Forget God's Amazing Love;
For he sent his only begotten Son from above
so that whoever believes in Him would not perish
but have Everlasting life and love.

Jesus left His place in heaven.
To come down here below
to show you how much He loves you
and to battle for your soul.

To ensure your place in heaven.
If only you'll believe.
The cross that He died to carry
He carried for you and me.

Once you receive Him into your heart
He always promised to be there.
He will never leave you nor forsake you
because that's how much He cares.

So, what are you waiting for?

Don't get Left Behind!

All you have to say is forgive me, Jesus
Come into my heart and be forever mine!

LOVE ONE ANOTHER

A new commandment I give to you, that you love one another; as I have loved you, that you also love one another. By this all will know that you are My disciples if you have love for one another.

JOHN 13:34–35

LOVE ONE ANOTHER

Why do we pull away from each other?
Why do we pull away from God?
Why do we build dividing walls?
What are we trying to hide?

When you receive Jesus as your Lord and Savior
you become my brother or sister in Christ.
No more walking all alone.
We'll be walking side by side.

If you fall down, I'll pick you up.
If you are sick, I'll hold your hand.
If someone seeks to destroy you
I will help you fight and make a stand.

No enemy can defeat us
if we're walking side by side.
As long as we love one another,
the enemy will run and hide.

We need each other through the good times,
We need each other through the bad.
We must show others Jesus' love
by walking hand in hand.

Life is too hard to walk alone;
that is a playground for the enemy to roam.
He enjoys being a bully,
beating you up and causing you pain.

Separating you from loved ones
is a trophy for his domain.

You're my brother, and you're my sister,
so, take me by the hand.
Let's walk together side by side
through this dry and thirsty land.

Let's get a fire going, for it only takes a spark!
For light removes evil and chases away the dark!

So, let your light shine brightly,
and stand for what is true.
Let your light shine brightly,
and the enemy will run from you.

You have one life, and it will soon pass.
But what you've done for Jesus,
will last and last!

JUST A STONE

A long time ago,
there was a young man.
That brought down a giant
with a rock in his hand!

God gave him the power
to bring this evil down,
because in his heart
God was found.

Now evil has risen again.
A spiritual evil has hit our land.
A change can begin
in a few short days
but it can't be done
unless we change our ways!

We have to humble ourselves and pray
and stand together in a powerful way.

Because no weapon will be strong enough.
No bomb will be big enough
unless God is back on the throne.

So, if we let God back into our Country
into our hearts and our Homes.
We can beat this thing with

JUST A STONE!

If My people who are called by My name will humble themselves, and pray and seek My face, and turn from their wicked ways, then I will hear from heaven, and will forgive their sin and heal their land.

2 Chronicles 7:14 (NKJV)

If you have never received Jesus Christ as your Lord and Savior, and you would like to, please say this Prayer of Salvation out loud to our Heavenly Father.

Say…Heavenly Father,

I ask You this day to forgive me of all of my sins.
I come boldly to the throne of God and
confess my sins before You.

I believe in my heart that Jesus died and rose again.
Because of what Jesus did on the Cross for me,
offering me this gift of salvation,
declaring His Amazing Love for me,
I gladly receive You now, Jesus, into my heart.
My past is behind me and Satan has no power over me.

Thank You for saving me.
I believe right now that I am saved.
I am a child of God.

I ask you today to write my name in the
Lamb's Book of Life.

And Heavenly Father, I want everything
You have to offer me.

I ask You to fill me with the Holy Spirit
so that I may be able
to withstand the enemy and live the life
You created me to live.

I ask this in Jesus' Name,

Amen.

Milton Keynes UK
Ingram Content Group UK Ltd.
UKHW051112090224
437489UK00007B/19

9 798890 417725